Original title:
The Call of the Sea Turtle

Copyright © 2025 Creative Arts Management OÜ
All rights reserved.

Author: Beckett Sinclair
ISBN HARDBACK: 978-1-80587-302-0
ISBN PAPERBACK: 978-1-80587-772-1

(Freedom in the Waves)

In the ocean's embrace, they glide with glee,
Wobbling and bobbing, so wild and free.
With shells like a car, they cruise on by,
Flip-flopping like dancers, beneath the sky.

Their flippers are wings, in a watery race,
Chasing their dreams at a laid-back pace.
While seaweed confetti flows with the tide,
These quirky old turtles just want to ride.

With laughter and bubbles, they brighten the floor,
Cracking coded jokes with each gentle shore.
"Who needs a surfboard? We're perfect," they grin,
Splashing in circles, let the giggles begin.

From coral to caverns, they never look stressed,
Making friends with the fish, they simply jest.
With all of their charm, they take quite a bow,
For freedom in waves—that's their fun, and here's how!

Guardians of Glistening Shores

Beneath the sun, they flipper-flap,
In silly circles, they take a nap.
With shades on eyes, they savor the light,
Guardians of sand, oh what a sight!

Shells like boats on a frothy spree,
Turning cartwheels, as happy as can be.
They slip and slide, creating a show,
With laughter echoing where breezes blow.

Wayfarers of the Endless Horizon

Yo-ho-ho, the waves do tease,
Sailing through currents with buttery ease.
Navigators of seaweed and foam,
Finding lost treasures, they call it home.

With winks and giggles, they chart their course,
In a rubbery dance, with a splash of force.
They joust with jellyfish, twirl with glee,
Splendid explorers of the deep blue sea!

The Tide's Eternal Melody

Clap your flippers, join the band,
A symphony played on the golden sand.
Waves that rhythm, turtles in tune,
Bouncing with joy 'neath the bright, round moon.

Laughing and splashing, a chorus takes flight,
Songs of the ocean, sparkling and bright.
With every plunge, their spirits soar,
Dancing through tides, forevermore.

Trails of the Ocean's Keepers

In trails of bubbles, the fun begins,
Finding old flip-flops, laughing like twins.
With each little splash, they leave a mark,
Guiding lost sailors, bright as a spark.

Shells tell stories of mischief and play,
Under the sun, they frolic all day.
Through shimmering waters, they wiggle and twist,
Laughter and joy, impossible to resist!

Harmonies in the Ocean's Belly

In the sea's dance, shells do prance,
A turtle sings, in a comical trance.
With a splash and a flip, no care in the tide,
Jellyfish giggle, their secrets can't hide.

Seagulls snicker from high above,
While crabs on the sand play tag and shove.
Every wave whispers a chuckling tune,
As turtles trot under the silver moon.

Tranquil Journeys of the Blue Realm

A slow-motion chase, what a sight to find,
Seaweed wigs on turtles, oh so unrefined!
They're racing the fish, but just having fun,
While starfish cheer from their rocky bun.

Flip-flop and flop, they'll dance through the foam,
Swapping tales of their watery home.
With a wink and a wave, they float quite free,
In a world where laughter is key to the sea.

An Odyssey Eclipsed by Waves

Under bright bubbles, turtle leaps high,
With fish in formations, they wiggle and fly.
The ocean erupts in a giggling cheer,
As dolphins toast drinks, splashing good cheer.

Clownfish tell jokes, in a coral parade,
While turtles just muddle, in their capers displayed.
Fishes with fins have a dance party thrive,
In this underwater laugh-a-thrive dive!

Guardians of the Aquatic Dream

With a shell like a boat, they navigate seas,
Turtles don sunglasses, catching the breeze.
They've got tales of the deep, of ruckus and glee,
In their watery kingdom, they just love to be.

Flippers on deck, they take a grand stand,
Hosting a party on the bright sandy strand.
Little fish join, their scales all aglow,
As turtles enthrall with their oceanic show.

Tidal Stories Etched in Sand

A turtle winks at the rising sun,
Spinning tales of ocean fun.
With a snack of seaweed on the go,
He dances in waves, putting on a show.

Shells and crabs join the jolly feast,
Belly flops and laughter, never ceased.
They race with dolphins, what a grand sight,
While seagulls cackle, trying to take flight.

Guardians of Oceans Unseen

In depths so blue, a party raves,
A wise old turtle plays with the waves.
He wears a crown of coral bright,
Making fish laugh, oh, what a sight!

His buddies tease with silly jokes,
While jellyfish twirl in bubble strokes.
They share a snack of popcorn shells,
In secret spots where ocean dwells.

The Soft Footprints of Time

With flippers wide, he strolls the shore,
Leaving footprints, he hopes for more.
A hermit crab has joined the game,
Poking fun, calling out his name.

They ponder life with gentle cheer,
In the salty breeze, singing clear.
Time whispers laughter in the air,
As the turtle twirls without a care.

Solitude in the Blue Depths

Beneath the waves, a turtle grins,
Searching for fun, where the sea begins.
He tells the fish, "Don't be so shy!"
We can twirl and play, just you and I!

A conch shell rolls, it joins the fun,
As underwater races have begun.
With swirls of bubbles, and giggles too,
In the blue depths, there's always something new.

Embrace of the Salty Breeze

Beneath the sun, they wiggle and sway,
In the ocean's dance, they're always at play.
With shells on their backs, they take a long ride,
Laughing at waves that crash with their tide.

They wear sunglasses, a hat for the heat,
Surfing the waves, isn't that neat?
Chasing their friends, oh what a delight,
In the salty embrace that feels just right.

Dance of the Tortoises

In a conga line, they shimmy along,
Wobbling and giggling, singing their song.
Flip-flops on flippers, they shuffle and glide,
Making a splash, as they dance with pride.

They twirl 'round coral, in a dance-off spree,
"Let's see your moves!" calls one from the sea.
With shells shining bright, and laughter so loud,
These tortoises dance, majestic and proud.

Graceful Swimmers of the Sea

With fins like a glide, they move through the blue,
Graceful and swift, like they've got a clue.
"Watch my pirouette!" one shouts with a cheer,
While spinning and twirling without any fear.

In synchronized patterns, they twirl and they twist,
Creating a ballet you shouldn't have missed.
They giggle and splash, letting out such fun,
These elegant swimmers, racing the sun.

Ancient Paths Crisscross the Currents

Through currents and tides, they chart every way,
With maps in their shells, they navigate play.
"Next stop, the reef!" one exclaims with delight,
As they journey together, morning 'til night.

Winding through waters, the stories unfold,
Of adventures encountered, both brave and bold.
With laughter and friendship, their paths intertwine,
These travelers of waves, living life so fine.

Whispers of the Ocean's Guardian

Upon the shore she sneaks and glides,
With flippers wide, she surely hides.
A shell-shaped disco ball of dreams,
She sways and twirls in ocean streams.

All the fish just stop and stare,
She sports a hat with ocean flair.
"Catch me if you can!" she quips,
As seaweed dances 'round her hips.

With every dive, a splash she makes,
A giggling greeting for the wakes.
Bubbles flutter, laughter streams,
In playful waves, she spins her themes.

Her shell is art, a funky sight,
A technicolor dream at night.
The ocean sings, her friends all cheer,
The razzle-dazzle turtle's here!

Journey of a Shelled Voyager

On sandy trails, she drags along,
With silly strut, she sings her song.
Her travel bag? Just seaweed snacks,
And dreams of ocean's fun-filled hacks.

A wave rolls in, she takes a leap,
But oh dear! She lands in a heap.
Her friends giggle with glee and jest,
While she claims she's just taking rest.

Her navigation's quite the mess,
She ends up wearing a coral dress.
"Not what I planned!" she flails with grace,
Like a star at an awkward space race.

Yet through the blunders and the laughs,
She gathers tales like ocean drafts.
With every journey, wise and spry,
She waves her shell and says goodbye!

Beneath the Waves, a Heart Beats

Underwater tales of mirth await,
Our turtle turns, why hesitate?
With a heart so light, she dives with flair,
Scheduling fun in the salty air.

She twirls with jellyfish, quite a show,
Imitating their bouncy flow.
"Look at me!" she proudly beams,
As laughter ripples through the streams.

Nudging crabs with playful pokes,
While cracking jokes with friendly folks.
Her antics bring a cheerful spark,
Running laps in the ocean park.

When evening falls, she grins and yawns,
Dreaming of more silly dawns.
The sea embraces, laughter swells,
In joy, she weaves her shimm'ring spells!

Echoes from the Coral Kingdom

In the coral palace, she rules the roost,
With a crown of shells, she's always juiced.
"Who needs armor? I'm the queen!"
Her giggles bounce, a playful scene.

Her subjects swirl, the fish all cheer,
"Make way for the turtle, bring her near!"
She leads parades with a flip and a spin,
Celebrating chaos, let the fun begin!

In the royal reef, where colors pop,
They dance to the rhythm, nonstop.
With sea cucumbers as her crew,
She orchestrates that wild blue view.

As currents fade and night sets in,
She shares a tale with a hearty grin.
In the coral kingdom, joy abounds,
With every splash, love resounds!

Voyagers on the Water's Edge

We waddle like pros on the sandy shore,
Two flippers in sync, who could ask for more?
With shells on our backs, we slide down with glee,
It's a slippery ride for a turtle like me.

Oh look, there's a crab with a dance in his step,
We join in the fun, it's a shell-upset prep.
We're kings of the beach, no worries in sight,
Until a kid runs by, oh what a fright!

The sun beats down hard, we take a nice nap,
Might dream of seaweed or a fishy mishap.
From dawn until dusk, we bask in the glow,
Then midnight comes calling, it's off we must go.

As waves roll in, we ride with delight,
Turtle Party Central, what a wild night!
Under the stars, we share turtle tales,
With laughter and joy, we spin our own sails.

The Timeless Rhythm of the Sea

Waves crashing gently, it's a turtle ballet,
We twirl in the water, just dancing away.
With shells so polished, we're ready to glide,
In time with the rhythm, the ocean our guide.

We chat with the fish as they swim on by,
"Have you seen my cousin? He's really shy!"
A dolphin suggests, "Let's race to the rock!"
But wait, is that lunch? Oh, let's have a talk!

The sun's setting low, we're spinning in play,
Oh dear, we flip over, what a clumsy display!
With laughter erupting, we float on our backs,
Giggles erupt as we dodge all the hacks.

Moonshine is bright; we pull off some pranks,
As seagulls complain, we give them some thanks.
Being a turtle is simply the best,
With laughter and joy, we never take rest.

Essence of the Ocean Wanderers

Under the waves, we shimmy and shake,
Each turtle in tow, what a silly mistake!
With bubbles to giggle, we frolic and swirl,
Through coral and kelp, we twirl and we whirl.

Our friends are the fish, each a quirky chap,
They swim in a line, then fall in a nap.
But we're on a quest, for the biggest of snacks,
It's seaweed for lunch, just don't look for cracks.

A blowfish puffs up, it's quite the grand scene,
"Why so serious?" we chuckle between.
The ocean's our stage, the world's full of wonder,
With laughter and fun, we'll never feel under.

As sunset approaches, we gather and chat,
Spinning funny tales, and how we got fat!
We'll treasure these moments, so silly and bright,
Living the turtle way, in pure, joyful light.

Sheltered in the Sea's Secrets

In the kelp forest maze, we weave and we bob,
When a sea star dives past, it gives me the job.
"Let's find the treasure, I just heard it glint!"
With giggles and flippers, we're no time to squint.

A toothless old turtle shares stories anew,
Of grand snatches of pearls and a fish with a shoe.
We roll on the sand, as legends unfold,
But is that true? Or just tales that he told?

The ocean's our home, it soothes every fear,
While dodging the gulls that come swooping near.
With shells all a-jingling, we pull a parade,
Our quirky procession, as laughter's conveyed.

Under the moonlight, we bask in delight,
Waving fins to our friends, we dance through the night.
Guardians of joy, with secrets to spare,
In the endless blue, we'll always be there.

Born from the Waves' Embrace

In a shell, snug and round,
A turtle spins without a sound.
He wears a grin, all bright and sly,
Under the sun, he waves goodbye.

With flippers flapping, oh what a sight,
He dances through the morning light.
Friends in coral, they cheer and shout,
"Hey, slowpoke! It's time to route!"

A jellyfish floats, in our way we crash,
He shrinks and quivers, what a splash!
With laughter bubbling all around,
Who knew such joy in sea could be found?

From the waves, our troubles released,
As fishy jokes form a comedy feast.
Born of fun, we flip and glide,
In this playful tide, we take our ride.

Travelers of the Crystal Waters

Under the waves, we roam so free,
Each little turtle has a decree.
"Adventure awaits in the azure sea!"
So we flip and twirl with glee.

Through kelp forests, we zip and zoom,
Dodging crabs in their sandy room.
An octopus winks, with a glint in his eye,
"Catch me if you can!" he says, oh my!

We munch on algae, a salad divine,
As bubbles gurgle, this life is fine.
In the depths where the sunbeams dance,
We twirl in a circle, what a chance!

Travelers bold on a slippery quest,
Sharing laughs and joy, it's simply the best.
With each stroke, our spirits lift,
In the crystal waters, we find our gift.

Riddles of the Undersea World

Why did the fish blush in the reef?
He saw a turtle, oh what a relief!
"Do you think I'm pretty?" it cheekily quipped,
While the turtle just grinned and swiftly skipped.

Pufferfish puzzles make us scratch our heads,
"Does he eat burgers or prefers fish spreads?"
In currents of laughter, we find our way,
Solving riddles while we sway.

A dolphin giggles, flipping high,
"Why do you turtles never fly?"
We shrug and chuckle, keeping it light,
"Because our style's all about delight!"

In this underwater circus, we play and tease,
Sharing our jokes with the playful breeze.
Riddles ripple through waves of fun,
In our world of laughter, we're never done.

Fade into the Blue

As the sun sets, colors blend,
Our turtle gang knows how to transcend.
In the twilight, we start to sway,
A perfect end to a busy day.

With a flip, we twirl in a bubbly spree,
Racing shadows, oh what glee!
"Last one in's a soggy shoe!" we cheer,
Then dive down low, without a fear.

The coral glows in the fading light,
Each brush of water, a tickle, a bite.
With laughter echoing through the deep,
We drift away, into dreams we'll seep.

Under the stars, the ocean hums,
As we fade into night, hear the sea drum.
In silly moments, our hearts take flight,
In the vast blue world, everything's just right.

Echoes of the Tides

In cozy nests beneath the sand,
They roll and tumble, oh so grand!
With flippers flapping, they start to slide,
Chasing waves with a silly pride.

Old shells whisper tales so bright,
Of goofy dances under moonlight.
With every splash, they giggle away,
Who knew the ocean liked to play?

They chase the crabs with little glee,
But those sly critters flee with a plea.
'The tide's on my side,' the turtle thinks,
As they plot their next oceanic jinx.

Bubbles rise with cheerful sounds,
In aquatic antics, joy abounds.
On this watery stage, they perform with flair,
Who knew the sea could be so rare?

Shells and Dreams

In a world of shells, they strut with pride,
Wearing a coat of ocean's tide.
With every wave, they twist and twirl,
Living large in a saltwater swirl.

They peek at crabs, with wince and grin,
'You can't catch me!' oh, where to begin?
With each wild leap, they slip and slide,
Abandoning worries, setting dreams wide.

From sunrise to sunset, laughter rides,
As they zoom through kelp, bumping sides.
Swirling whiskers, bright ocean beams,
Living life with whimsical dreams.

So if you're near where the waters gleam,
Look for the turtles lost in a dream.
Giggles ring out as they speed away,
In a world of wonder, come laugh and play!

The Voyage of the Ancient Ones

Old turtles glide with wisdom's grace,
Yet love a good chase and a playful race.
With wrinkled skin and backstories galore,
Each flip and flop, a chance to explore.

They navigate reefs like clever old spies,
While plotting a prank with mischievous eyes.
In shadows they sneak, then pop out with flair,
Causing a stir with the fish, oh beware!

The ocean's their tapestry, woven with fun,
As they journey through ripples, diving 'til done.
With tales to share, like legends at sea,
They laugh and they sing, 'Come join us, be free!'

Through currents and whirlpools, they boldly swim,
Stealing the show with a flip and a whim.
Ancient and clever, they soar with delight,
In a watery canvas, their spirit takes flight.

Serenity in the Deep Blue

Under waves, they dance with glee,
Life's a party in the blue sea!
With every bubble, a giggle escapes,
'Take a swim, don't care about shapes!'

Past coral gardens, they scatter and glide,
With clumsy moves and a joyful stride.
A whirl here and there, it's all in good fun,
While sunbeams teem like a tropical run.

With dolphins diving in the wake,
They join the ballet, for joy's own sake.
On this grand stage, all creatures unite,
Spreading laughter from morn until night.

So here's to the turtles, masters of cheer,
Bringing sunshine and giggles to those far and near.
In the vast, vibrant blue, they reign supreme,
Swimming through life, it's all a grand dream!

Tales from the Coral's Edge

Down by the reef where the colors gleam,
The turtles joke while they swim and dream.
With fins like flippers, they glide with glee,
"Why did the fish cross? To laugh with me!"

They twirl in the water, a dance so spry,
Chasing their shadows as they swoop by.
A crab on a rock scoffs with a huff,
"Stop swimming so fast, can't get enough!"

The octopus giggles with eight arms at play,
Saying, "I can't keep up, so, hey, let's ballet!"
But turtles are sly, turning back for some fun,
A race through the bubbles, oh, what a run!

As sunset paints skies in soft orange hues,
They gather together to share silly news.
With tales of the currents, they chuckle and snort,
A troop of old friends in their underwater court.

Reflections Beneath the Surface

In the blue depths, a turtle gave a wink,
"Look at my shell, what do you think?"
His buddy replied with a flick of his tail,
"You've got more style than a sea snail!"

They drift with the waves, making quite the scene,
"Is that a seaweed hat? Oh, you mean—green!"
Laughing at bubbles that tickle their chins,
They ponder if jellyfish ever do wins.

A dolphin nearby starts doing a flip,
"Why do you turtles move at that clip?"
"No rush in this ocean, we're here for a laugh,"
"Join us gracefully, don't make a gaffe!"

Together they twirl, a swirling brigade,
Making a splash in their goofy parade.
As laughter echoes through the coral bright,
The sea is their stage, oh, what a sight!

Vessel of Oceanic Reflection

Upon the seafloor, the turtles convene,
In a circle they sit, like a marine cuisine.
One whispered, "Oi, has anyone seen,
The fish that thought he was super slim?"

They giggled aloud, imagining the scene,
A fish in a tux, thinking he's keen.
"I'd swim faster too if I had a bow tie,"
Said another while watching a seagull fly by.

"Do you think they can swim?"

"Not with those wings,"
Rumbled the current, as it started to sing.
Their shells caught the light like a mid-afternoon feast,
A safe place for laughter, where joy is released.

From ripples to giggles, they traveled along,
With tales of the tides, they felt very strong.
As the sun slipped away, painted the sea,
They laughed and they danced, just happy to be!

The Gentle Glide

In tranquil waters, where the rhythm flows,
The turtles glide with grace, as everyone knows.
"Why don't we race?" one boldly proposed,
"No hurry, dear friend, let's just strike a pose!"

With an elegant twist, and a flick of the fin,
"Look at us shine, now, that's how we win!"
A shout from the depths echoed, filled with delight,
"Hold your turtles!—We might lose track of night!"

They rolled through the kelp, in a silly parade,
As stars twinkled down, their worries betrayed.
"Let's snack on some seagrass!" said one with a grin,
"We'll feast like kings and then call it a win!"

As giggles resounded, the day turned to night,
In the moonlit waters, they twinkled with light.
With a splash and a laugh, they swam side by side,
In the heart of the ocean, where friendship won't hide.

Harmonies of the High Seas

Underwater disco, bubbles in a twirl,
Fish in tuxedos, ready to unfurl.
Turtles in shades, do the funky glide,
Krill doing the worm, with a joyful ride.

Shy sea urchins giggle, hiding in a shell,
Chuckling otters join in, weaving a spell.
The currents are the beats, the waves keep time,
As crabs tap dance, all in perfect rhyme.

With seaweed confetti floating in the breeze,
In this underwater party, everyone's at ease.
Jellyfish are the lights, glowing wild and bright,
This ocean's a rave, everything feels right.

So grab your flippers, come and join the fun,
In the briny deep, frolic till we're done.
Each splash a giggle, each wave a cheer,
Underwater shenanigans, oh so dear!

Secrets Lurking in the Liquid Depths

Whispers of pirates, secrets in the foam,
Turtles spinning tales, far away from home.
Fins flapping stories of treasures and more,
A crab with a map, searching for the shore.

An octopus giggles as he draws in the sand,
Sketching out adventures, oh isn't it grand?
A dolphin named Dave, with a wry little grin,
Plays hide-and-seek, letting the games begin.

The whispers get louder, as mermaids appear,
With glittering tails, they bring laughter and cheer.
Are they some treasure, or just flowers of the sea?
We'll keep it a secret, just you and me.

Every bubble a giggle, every wave a jest,
In the deep blue abyss, we're truly blessed.
So dive in my friend, don't swim too fast,
For secrets unfold, when the fun's unsurpassed!

The Solace of Swells and Shores

On sandy beaches, turtles take the stage,
Wiggling and jiggling, setting the age.
Surfboards made of coral, rides are supreme,
Dolphins do flips, living the dream.

Seashells play maracas, clacking in delight,
As the tides hum songs, under the moonlight.
Turtles bring cupcakes for a fancy buffet,
While seagulls dance, don't let them fly away!

Starfish make wishes, plucking from the sea,
Singing sweet songs, harmoniously free.
A playful sea breeze, tickles our toes,
As laughter erupts, the joy only grows.

With the sun setting down, it's the end of our spree,
But every seaside adventure, we hold tightly.
Beneath the waves, where laughter takes flight,
The ocean keeps dancing, heartwarming and bright!

Guardians of the Ocean Whisper

Guardians of bliss, in shells snug and tight,
Whispering secrets under the moonlight.
A turtle named Gus with a goofy grin,
Performs his deep dives, and beams from within.

Crabs hold a meeting, with pinchers in the air,
Discussing how to catch the best tasty fare.
While sea stars gossip, twinkling with mirth,
Sharing the news of the latest underwater birth.

The wise old whale sings a lullaby sweet,
As fish gather 'round for a melody treat.
The ocean a canvas, colors vibrant and bold,
In this underwater circus, life never gets old.

So swim with the currents, dance in the waves,
For guardians are watching, the joyful ones that saves.
With laughter and wonder, we cherish this ride,
In the arms of the ocean, forever our guide!

The Enchanted Path of the Seafarer

In shells of sun and salty breeze,
A turtle slips with humor, if you please.
With flippers wide, it makes a splash,
Whispering tales of a seaweed stash.

Oh, what a journey through foamy sprays,
Chasing fish with bewildered gaze.
Bubbles pop as laughter flows,
In this watery world, anything goes!

A flip and a flop, a glide and a grin,
Each wave they ride is a chance to win.
But watch out! Here comes a jellyfriend,
It jiggles and wiggles, this party won't end.

With barnacles dancing, a quirky sight,
The marine circus is pure delight.
Join the fun, take off your shoes,
In this ocean realm, it's hard to lose!

Moonlit Melodies of the Marine Sage

Under the moon, a turtle sings,
Melodies drifting on gentle wings.
With seaweed hair and a jolly dance,
It twirls through waves like a summer romance.

Each note it croons brings laughter and cheer,
Fish gather 'round, they lend an ear.
A starfish claps its tiny hands,
Joining the party in moonlit sands.

The ocean's a stage for this merry show,
Sea cucumbers sway, putting on a glow.
"Let's boogie!" they shout with giddy delight,
Waving to dolphins, oh what a night!

As dawn approaches, the tunes fade away,
Still, they chuckle 'til the end of the day.
With hearts so light and full of glee,
Who knew that the ocean would be so free?

Driftwood Memories and Oceanic Realms

On driftwood logs, the turtles play,
Balancing snacks that float their way.
With a flick of a fin and giggling shells,
They invent games with ocean spells.

"Catch the crab!" one shouts with pride,
While hermit crabs scurry, side by side.
But watch out for seagulls, sneaky and sly,
They dive for the treats as they laugh and cry.

Old shells tell stories of days gone past,
As turtles share giggles that seem to last.
With each tiny splash, a memory made,
In this driftwood kingdom, joy will not fade.

So gather 'round, dear ocean friends,
With silly tales, the laughter never ends.
In a world where the sun and sea intertwine,
Even seaweed chuckles, "Life is just fine!"

Echoing the Rhythm of the Reef

In coral gardens, rhythms abound,
A turtle grooves with a silly sound.
"Do the waddle!" calls out a brave shrimp,
As they dance beneath the waves, not a blimp.

With a splash and a wiggle, they form a train,
Nudibranchs join, adding to the gain.
"Oh look, a parade!" the clownfish beam,
What a hilarious underwater dream!

With laughter bouncing off the coral walls,
Every fishy friend, heed the calls.
A conch shell starts to beat its tune,
While turtles twirl beneath the silver moon.

As the party swells in a peppy beat,
Seashells dig in, enjoying the treat.
Come one, come all, in joy you'll thrive,
In this zany world, we all come alive!

A Dance with the Deep Blue

With flippers wide, they twirl and twist,
In a waltz so grand, they can't resist.
Bubbles rise as they giggle with glee,
Who knew the ocean was a jamboree?

Jellyfish float like fancy balloons,
While fish join in, singing silly tunes.
Spinning around in a watery ballet,
Their goofy grace makes waves all day.

Sand dollars cheer from the sandy floor,
As turtles show off, wanting more and more.
A conga line forms, how funny to see,
A party beneath, where everyone's free.

Under the sun, their laughter does ring,
In a world of wonder, where all are king.
With corny jokes and a splashy delight,
They dance together, hearts so light!

Shellbound Secrets of the Abyss

In a hidden cove with brightly colored shells,
Turtles giggle over the secrets that dwells.
An octopus whispers a riddle so fine,
While seaweed tickles, making them pine.

With mischievous winks, they spin their lore,
Chasing crabs who dance on the ocean floor.
Their shells like hats, all fancy and bright,
"Is this fashion? Or a funny sight?"

A clownfish watches, cracking up loud,
As turtles parade like a circus crowd.
With each silly tale and a splash of cheer,
These shellbound secrets bring everyone near.

They trade funny sayings in bubbles around,
Making all the sea life burst out in sound.
With joy in the depths and laughter's caress,
The abyss reveals its whimsical mess.

Tideborne Tales of Resilience

On the waves that roll, the turtles play,
With tales of adventure, brightening the day.
"Remember the time we rode the big swell?"
They giggle and chuckle, oh what a tale to tell!

Through storms they've surfed and whirlpools spun,
Adventures so wild, say, 'Aren't we just fun?'
With shells like boats, they journey along,
Making up verses, where all sing a song.

When they find a lost shoe, they start a parade,
"Whose fancy footwear has thus been way laid?"
A sea turtle's humor is truly the best,
Sailing through life without any rest.

So raise up a fin for the tideborne crew,
Whose laughter echoes in waters so blue.
With each twist and turn in their watery quest,
They show resilience, and humor, and jest.

Navigating Celestial Currents

Beneath the starlit, shimmering waves,
Turtles take off, as if they're all knaves.
On currents of laughter, they glide and they swirl,
With dreams in their hearts, giving ocean a whirl.

"Follow the moon! It's a neon route!"
They scream with delight, feeling astute.
Dodging the jellyfish, they giggle with cheer,
In this celestial dance, nothing to fear.

The constellations shine overhead,
Guiding their journey as they're being led.
With each little bump, they just burst out in glee,
Navigating joy is the key to be free.

In the midnight waters, where starlight does meet,
Turtles learn secrets, oh so sweet.
With tales from the depths and dreams of the tall,
They sail through the cosmos, laughing with all!

The Silent Odyssey of the Tortoise

In the ocean's warm embrace, they glide,
With a waddle, they take a ride.
Shells glisten in the bright sunlight,
Chasing fish with all their might.

They ponder life at a leisurely pace,
While crabs scuttle, a lively race.
With every flip, they laugh and cheer,
What a sight, oh, how we revere!

They hold wisdom in their slow move,
Yet dance like they're in a groove.
With jellyfish, they share a laugh,
"Don't touch me now, just take the path!"

When evening falls, they gather round,
To tell the tales of where they've found.
Each story drips with salty glee,
For every wave, a new entry!

Serenity in Saltwater Dreams

Bubbles rise like giggles in the sea,
Underwater parties, oh so carefree!
With flippers flapping to the beat,
They boogie on corals, feeling the heat.

Surfing the waves like pros on a board,
Chasing a shadow, they laugh and hoard.
The seaweed tangles, a mischievous friend,
A ticklish moment, they don't want to end.

At sunrise, they sip on the ocean's brew,
Sipping salt and foam, a morning view.
All together, they share a feast,
Life is better with a crustacean lease!

In deep nest chambers, they rest with cheer,
Whispering secrets, drifting near.
While stars above illuminate the night,
These jolly turtles dream till the light!

Guardians of the Tide's Embrace

With shades of green, they roam the bay,
Leaving little footprints in soft gray.
"Who's that waddling?" the fish all snicker,
"Slow but steady, let's hope they flicker!"

They wear their shells like a knight's pride,
Swinging their heads from side to side.
In currents strong, they strike a pose,
"Look at us, with seaweed clothes!"

A dance with dolphins, a twirl here and there,
While seagulls squawk without a care.
"Hey, let's synchronize our little moves!
Who knew this ocean could host such groves?"

When the sun dips low, they bid adieu,
To tales long spun and shared anew.
They guard the tide with jokes and fun,
A tight-knit crew, under the sun!

Soliloquy of a Wayward Wanderer

With a turtle's heart, I roam the sea,
In search of adventures, oh so free!
I drift with the currents, feel the breeze,
Telling tales to the jellyfish with ease.

Every wave brings a story to tell,
Of starry nights where the sea creatures dwell.
"Oh look, an octopus!" I cry, it grins,
As we navigate the whirl of fins.

The moonlight dances, casting shadows bright,
With playful dolphins, I ride the night.
Together we jump, we swim, we swirl,
In this vast blue world, we twirl and twirl.

As dawn breaks softly and dreams fade away,
I ponder my journey, what will it say?
"A wanderer at heart, I'll forever glide,
This sea, my friend, is my joyful ride!"

The Language of the Waves

In a shell with a smile, they roam the sea,
Flippers waving hello, as bright as can be.
They dance with the currents and flip with delight,
Making fish giggle in the soft morning light.

With their friends, the seaweed, they frolic and play,
Telling tales of the ocean, come join in the fray.
"Did you see that big crab? He was doing the twist!"
And the jellyfish laughed, swaying with a flick.

Breaking out the shells, it's a musical jam,
With seagull grooves that make everyone pram.
So gather 'round, mates, for a swim and a song,
The sea's a big dance floor; come join, you belong!

The waves give a wink, with a twist and a swirl,
As turtles dive in with a splash and a whirl.
Their journeys are silly, their laughter sincere,
In the vast, silly sea, there's no need for fear.

Journeys Through the Blue Abyss

Beneath the waves, what a curious sight,
A turtle named Timmy, with goggles so tight.
He paddles around with a laugh and a cheer,
"I can see all the fish! They're just tickling, dear!"

He tried to catch bubbles, but oh, what a mess,
Instead, he made friends, and they laughed in excess.
"Let's ride on a wave!" cried the young turtle crew,
With a flip and a splash, they painted the blue.

They played in the coral, like kids in a park,
Keeping their secrets till night, till it's dark.
But the octopus peeked, with an eye or two wide,
"Are those turtles just swimming, or are they high-tide?"

Through circles and curls, they whirled and they spun,
Drawing laughter from dolphins, oh, what a fun!
In the depths of the ocean, where bubbles do gleam,
Their joy is the treasure, their life is a dream.

Whispers of the Undersea Dream

In the moon's soft glow, turtles gather at night,
Exchanging their tales, what a whimsical sight!
"I once met a fish who just wouldn't stop chatting,
He had so much gossip, it was simply flatting!"

They giggled at the crabs who danced with delight,
In their little claw-taps, they brought pure delight.
"I swear, they would boast, 'We're the kings of the beach!'
While skipping and hopping, oh, such laughter to reach!"

From currents to eddies, they twirled like a dance,
In the great undersea, they gave friendship a chance.
"Watch out for the divers! They wear heavy suits,
But if you just giggle, they'll run like their hoots!"

For the moments are fleeting, so sprinkle with glee,
In the chorus of bubbles, let your spirit be free.
With flippers and shells, let the waves weave a tale,
Of friendship and laughter in the bright, blue gale.

Echoes of the Ancient Waters

In depths of green, where the sea grasses sway,
Turtles laugh deeply, in their turtle ballet.
With a wink of their eyes and a flip of their tails,
They're swimming through stories and ancient fish trails.

They jest with the seals in a playful debate,
"Who can catch the most bubbles, my fishy mate?"
With a splash and a giggle, they dive down for fun,
Mapping maps with their flippers, under the sun.

When the starfish applauded, they took a grand bow,
To the claps of the shells and the waves' playful vow.
"May the sea always echo with laughter and play,
For life's like the tides, it sweeps us away."

As the sunlight is fading, they share one last cheer,
For the friendships they've made in the ocean, so dear.
With a swish and a laugh, they glide off to rest,
In the embrace of the sea, they truly are blessed.

Footprints in the Sand of Antiquity

In the sand, a turtle waddles,
A plump little boss in our coastal huddles.
With flippers wide, they dance and sway,
Tripping on crabs, come watch them play.

Shells on their back, oh what a sight,
Stumbling 'round in the moon's soft light.
They wink at fish, who giggle and tease,
As turtles strike poses with laughable ease.

The tide brings snacks, a feast they adore,
But they're picky eaters, that's for sure!
Seaweed and sushi, not quite the plan,
"Hold the kelp!" they say, "I'm not a fan!"

Ancient they are, with stories to share,
Of underwater shenanigans, oh what a flair!
So next time you wander through golden grains,
Just follow the laughter that fills the lanes.

A Journey of Shells and Stars.

A turtle sets forth on a shell-studded road,
Navigating with flair, they've quite the code.
Stars in their eyes, and shells in their pack,
They're the kings of the beach, and that's a fact!

"Oh look at me, I'm traveling far!"
They exclaim to the seagulls, who think they're a star.
While dodging the waves, they giggle with glee,
Who knew that the sea had such comedy?

Miracles happen on this sandy spree,
Pinching a jellyfish, "Oops! Sorry, buddy!"
They stumble and tumble, make such a fuss,
Even the crabs join in on the bus!

At the pier, they stop for a jellyfish snack,
Saying, "Hey there, pal, you're colorful, that's whack!"
With laughter and tales from dusk till dawn,
This is their journey, and they're never withdrawn.

Whispers of the Ocean's Guardian

Under the waves, a turtle retreats,
With a goofy grin and jiggly feats.
Flipping through currents, not a care in the world,\nA comet of green, just watch it twirl!

"Hey, little fish, I'm your big cousin,"
They shout with a chuckle, causing a buzzin'.
With a shell as their home, they twirl and glide,
Splashing the sea, all filled with pride.

At the coral disco, they bust a move,
"Watch this moment! I've got the groove!"
Fish swimming by laugh and cheer,
As the turtle shakes it from ear to ear.

Crabs join in with their sideways trot,
Each creature in sync, oh what a plot!
With echoes of laughter filling each swell,
The ocean's fun guardian, we know it so well.

A Journey Beneath Waves

Beneath the waves, the adventure awaits,
Where turtles clown around with their flippered mates.
They snicker at bubbles and hop on a shell,
"Come join the fun, it's quite the carousel!"

Flip-flopping around, they try to race,
But they trip on sea cucumbers, what a disgrace!
With a flip and a flop, they take a bow,
"Today's the day I'll be the best, wow!"

Finding lost treasures of pearly delight,
"Oh look, a fork! What a whimsical sight!"
They stash it for picnics, hidden away,
Planning a feast for a holiday play.

So if you hear laughter from deep in the sea,
Just know that it's turtles, and they're feeling free.
In their watery world, where joy fills the air,
They revel in giggles, with no time to spare.

Secrets Guarded by Shells

In the sandy arms where whispers dwell,
Each shell's a story, oh how they tell!
A gossiping crab with a cap on tight,
Tales of lost shoes and fish that bite.

The octopus winks with a mischievous grin,
Secrets of the deep, let the fun begin!
A starfish stumbles, oh what a fall,
"Who wants to dance?" it shouts to all!

The turtles giggle, racing the tide,
With shells like boats, they take their ride.
"Last one to shore buys a seaweed snack!"
As they flip and splash, there's no looking back.

Beneath the sun's giggle, the seafoam froths,
The ocean's a playground, and laughter floats.
With each wave crashing, the joy does swell,
In this world of whimsy, secrets guard shells.

The Lullaby of the Waves

The waves sing softly, a cheeky tune,
As turtles sway beneath the moon.
"Did you hear that joke?" one turtle grins,
"Why don't fish share? Because they're fins!"

The surf tickles toes in a playful way,
As seaweed giggles in the salty spray.
A flounder flops with a comical flair,
"Don't mind me, I'm just getting my hair!"

Clams clap their shells to the rhythm they make,
With a beat so catchy, you just can't shake.
The dolphins dance, twirling with ease,
As turtles add bubbles to all the tease.

In this ocean corner where laughter sings,
The waves keep rolling on joy's bright wings.
And as we drift with the tides' wavy hugs,
Life's a big joke beneath seaweed rugs.

Beneath the Moonlit Tide

Under the moon, a show begins,
With turtles diving and wearing grins.
"Catch me if you can!" they slyly shout,
As fish roll their eyes, "What's this about?"

The jellyfish jiggle, looking quite spry,
"Did you see my glow? I'm the star tonight!"
A remora tags along, just for the fun,
"Hold on tight while I try to run!"

Starfish play poker, with shells for bets,
"Anything beats a clam, no regrets!"
The tide pulls at laughter, a watery cheer,
As crabs tell tall tales we can barely hear.

So under the stars, they dance and play,
In the moonlit tide, they'll swim away.
Life's just a party with friends we find,
In the ocean's embrace, leave worries behind.

A Sojourn with the Giants

When turtles gather, it's quite a sight,
The grand old legends in the soft moonlight.
"Tell us your tales!" the hatchlings implore,
While the giants chuckle, "Oh, here's one more!"

"Back in my day, I was much faster,
With seaweed racing, I was a master!"
The eel just shrugs with a playful roll,
"Speed's not the game, it's to have a soul!"

They share silly moments, the past they weave,
With laughter that dances, it's hard to believe.
"Remember the time we escaped the net?
Oh, what a splash! I'll never forget!"

In this merry band, the giants proclaim,
Life's a big ocean, and laughter's the game.
With every new story, the night drifts on,
In a sojourn of joy, from dusk until dawn.

Gliding Through Forgotten Currents

In a shell that's stout and wide,
A turtle takes a silly ride,
Wobbling left, then swaying right,
Chasing fish who swim in fright.

With a grin that's slightly crooked,
Dodging crabs just like a good kid,
He flops and flares in ocean blue,
Forgetting chores, he's lost his cue.

Bubbles bloom with every glide,
As he tickles a fish that tried,
To hide behind the coral's flair,
But giggles spill through salty air.

So here's to turtles on their trail,
With flippers flapping, they set sail,
They teach us all to slow our pace,
And laugh a little in this space.

Heartbeats of a Blue Haven

On sunny days beneath the foam,
A turtle dreams of finding home,
Waving to a dolphin crew,
Who tease him with a peekaboo.

His heart beats loud in joyful song,
As seaweed sways and drifts along,
He spins around with flippers grand,
A disco ball in ocean land.

But watch out for the passing boat,
Where laughter mixes with a gloat,
Splashing sea with silly spins,
As turtles dance and fetch their fins.

With every wave comes new delight,
In waters warm and stars so bright,
A party hosted by the sea,
Where humor flows, wild and free.

The Enigma of Serenity

In tranquil seas of gentle tides,
A turtle smiles as he abides,
With a wisdom, oh so profound,
As jellyfish twirl all around.

He ponders life with squinty eyes,
While sea urchins wear their ties,
Dressed for brunch in coral mist,
He giggles, 'What is this, a twist?'

His friends convene for tea and fun,
Where laughter bubbles, never done,
They toast to squawks from seagulls bright,
While nibbling snacks, a pure delight.

So here's to peace in salty looks,
Where humor thrives in picture books,
For life's a jest beneath the tide,
In enchanted waves, we all abide.

A Path through the Tenebrous Waters

In shadows deep where stories dwell,
A turtle's tale begins to swell,
With a flashlight made of jellyfish,
He navigates his secret wish.

Through murky depths, he stumbles near,
Only to find a mermaid's cheer,
They giggle 'bout the things unseen,
As fish parade in mischievous green.

With every turn, a chuckle bursts,
As squids juggle and the sea firsts,
A dance of chaos in the night,
Where every twist brings pure delight.

So join the natives of this scene,
With turtles bright and laughs between,
In tenebrous waters, strange and grand,
Where humor floats in salty sand.

Migrations in the Moonlight

Under the moon, they waddle and roam,
With flippers flapping, they leave their foam.
A party of turtles, what a sight,
Dancing on waves, oh what a night!

Singing to crabs with a shimmery tune,
Trying to catch a ride on the moon.
They laugh at the stars, oh what a mess,
Wishing they'd packed a little more zest!

Flip-flopping dreams in the shimmering sea,
Fins in the air, they twirl with glee.
Who knew that turtles had such flair?
They twinkle and giggle, without a care!

With jellyfish jelly sliding like jam,
They plan their route, but oh, who gives a dam?
Crashing the reef for a midnight feast,
Those turtles are wild, to say the least!

A Dance with the Current

Curly tails and swirly shells,
Turtles surfing like oceanic elves.
With the current's swing, they twirl and glide,
Belly-flopping fish can't help but slide!

On seaweed dance floors, they show their skills,
Spinning like tops, chasing sweet thrills.
With a flip and a flop, they strike a pose,
While playful dolphins gossip and doze.

'Is that a tango or the cha-cha-cha?'
One turtle wonders, while munching on a straw.
They twinkled their toes on the coral's sway,
Stomping and laughing, all night and day!

When tired, they nap on a comfy spread,
Dreaming of parties in colorful beds.
The tide may come in and pull them away,
But they'll swim back to play another day!

The Shell's Whisper

In the still of the night, shells gather near,
Sharing tales of the ocean, full of cheer.
Cracking up jokes of their beachside quests,
With every whisper, laughter manifests.

'Hey, did you hear about the fish with the flair?
He put on a suit, but forgot his hair!'
Shells clink and chuckle, breaking the calm,
Echoes of laughter, soothing as balm.

Turtles in circles, gossiping wise,
With secrets of currents and fishy highs.
They plot their adventures, creating a stir,
Telling tales taller than waves that concur!

The moon grins down at this comical crew,
As shells share smack talks, like best friends do.
With a flick of their fins, submerging in mirth,
They hang tight together, for all they are worth!

Echoes in the Coral

Beneath the waves, where the corals glow,
Turtles relay tales with a funny flow.
'You won't believe the size of that snack!'
Amidst snickers and giggles, the stories unpack.

One turtle boasts of a jellyfish foe,
'He got tangled in seaweed, oh what a show!'
With bubbles of laughter, the ocean joins in,
Each wave is a chuckle, a soft gentle spin.

A crab slips and slides on the rocks in a dash,
Shouting, 'Hey turtles, stop making a splash!'
But turtles just dance on the coral's quick beat,
Wiggling and jiggling, oh isn't that neat?

With every echo, their friendship does swell,
Sharing the seas, they're under the spell.
From one coral reef to the next, they roam,
Together forever, they've found their home!

Memories of Oceans Past

Once swam a turtle with a shell so bright,
Thought it was a boat, gave fish a fright.
It tried to sail with the seagulls above,
But ended up tangled in jellyfish love.

With flippers flapping, it danced a jig,
In the middle of a trap, it felt quite big.
The crabs all laughed, with pinchers in applause,
As our swimmer sprawled on the sandy floors.

One day it wore a hat made of seaweed,
Strutting like a king, full of turtle creed.
The waves rolled in with a gentle tease,
"Is that a turtle, or just a light breeze?"

Now every wave brings a chuckle at night,
As memories rise, giving fish delight.
Each splash a giggle, every ripple a cheer,
For the silly turtle that swam without fear.

The Guardians' Rhythm

In the waves, the turtles kept the beat,
With flippers flaring, they danced in the heat.
A conga line that swayed with the tide,
Even the sharks couldn't help but glide.

They donned sombreros, and some wore shades,
Boogie-ing in bubbles, making spade charades.
An octopus DJ played tunes from afar,
With squishy beats, they'd go to the bar.

When the tides got rough, they'd spin and twirl,
Hitching a ride on a whirlpool's swirl.
The seagulls perched high, chortling in glee,
As their fishy friends danced beneath the sea.

And though they are guardians of all that's true,
They know how to party, our ocean crew.
With laughter and joy, they hold their sway,
In the rhythm of waters, they play all day.

Beneath the Surface's Soft Caress

A turtle named Timmy thought seagrass was cake,
Took a big bite, and gave the fish a shake.
With a mouthful of greens, he suddenly froze,
As a curious crab tapped his shell with a pose.

"Are you dining in style, or lost on your way?
You've mistaken your salad for food at a buffet!"
Timmy blinked twice, then let out a laugh,
"Guess I'll save room for a seaweed bath!"

Bubbles arose as he flipped and he spun,
Promising fishies a race just for fun.
They queued in a line, ready to dash,
With Timmy the turtle in a green, grassy splash.

Through kelp and coral, they zoomed with glee,
No worries or troubles beneath the blue sea.
In Timmy's world, every mismatch is neat,
A party of laughter, where life feels complete.

Legends of the Living Currents

In tales told by sea, there lives a tall tale,
Of a turtle who thought he was destined to sail.
With a map made of driftwood, he set out to roam,
But kept getting lost on the waves of foam.

"Just follow the fish!" his friends would advise,
But they moved too fast, like a watery prize.
He'd chase after bubbles, all shiny and bright,
And find himself stuck in a clam's little bite.

The legends that grow, of his goofy plight,
Echo through waters, twinkling at night.
With tales of adventures that never were drear,
All of the ocean giggles, "Oh dear!"

So here's to the swimmers who wander and play,
In currents that dance, let them lead the way.
With laughter and fun, they find their own track,
Every wave tells a story, there's never a lack.

Dreaming Under the Stars

Beneath the moon, we make our plans,
With turtle dreams in sandy lands.
They wink and wave with flippered grace,
In seaweed hats at a masquerade space.

Oh, what a sight, they dance with glee,
Chasing jellyfish like racing bees.
With shells so bright, they twirl and spin,
Laughing as if the fun won't thin.

They tell tales of waves and briny cheer,
As stars above wink, and the night is dear.
A party of turtles, oh what a show!
One tried to surf, but fell on his toe!

As dawn approaches, they bid goodnight,
With giggles that echo through morning light.
So here's to the turtles, wise and bold,
In dreams under stars, their tales unfold.

Born from the Ocean's Heart

From deep blue waters, they burst with flair,
Turtles emerge with a wobbly stare.
'What's this land?' one asks with a frown,
As others tumble and roll on down.

There's laughter and splashes all around,
As they hop and skip on the sandy ground.
With ocean breeze messing their hair,
One turtle claims he must shave with care!

Yet not a single one knows how to flip,
They trip and tumble, but never trip.
In sun suits made of bright sea moss,
They giggle and glide, they're the boss of gloss!

With shells so patterned, like polka dot fun,
They bury themselves for a quick little run.
From ocean's heart, with love and jest,
They rejoice in the sand, oh what a fest!

The Silent Voyage

On a raft of kelp, they glide and sway,
With silent giggles, they paddle away.
A tiny turtle gave a loud snore,
That echoed in waves, oh what a roar!

They sail through the sea with squeaks and squeals,
Avoiding the fish with their wiggly heels.
One tries to dive, but bounces right back,
With bubbles of laughter in his wake, what a track!

The moon above shines with silver glow,
While turtles dance like they're putting on a show.
With a wink and a nudge, they navigate light,
Finding laughs in the dark, oh what a sight!

Each wave is a pet, gentle and kind,
This silent voyage, forever entwined.
As laughter echoes over the brine,
These turtles embody the joy so divine!

Harmonies of the Blue Depths

In depths where the sun must do a little dive,
Turtles sing tunes that bring them alive.
With bubbles they blow, like a jazzy refrain,
They bop to the rhythm of the ocean's gain.

One turtle strummed on a shell of a clam,
Creating a serenade, oh what a jam!
Others joined in with a burble and chuckle,
In this underwater rock, none dare to buckle!

The octopus swayed with eight happy arms,
While a shrimp played triangle, bringing the charms.
Together they danced, a peculiar sight,
In harmonies sweet, they filled the night.

The waves applauded, their rhythm so grand,
With the turtles grooving all over the sand.
In blue depths so vivid, where fun never sweeps,
They share a melody, in tides that peep!

A Sheltered Pilgrim's Quest

A turtle set forth with a hopeful grin,
In search of a snack, let the feasting begin!
With seaweed in sight, it danced in delight,
But every small wave gave it quite a fright.

With flippers so grand, it styled a big splash,
Yet each tiny fish swam away in a dash.
"Where's my buffet?" it pondered in jest,
"I'll roll with the punches, I'm truly the best!"

It turned to the sun for a wise little tip,
"Why chase all the snacks when you could just skip?"
The dolphins just chuckled, they swam all around,
"Keep searching, dear friend, for what can be found!"

In a cozy nook, our traveler munched,
On a jellyfish snack that it accidentally crunched.
With laughter and joy, it shared a good cheer,
"I'm full of great laughs, now let's disappear!"

In the Embrace of the Endless

A turtle in shades, feeling quite suave,
Cruised with the waves like a hip, little star.
Its pals laughed and joked, "You should wear a crown!"
But the turtle just waved and didn't back down.

"It's a chill day today, I'll just float and glide,
Why rush to the shore when I can enjoy the ride?"
With a flip of its tail, the world was its stage,
A slow-motion dance as if turning a page.

It spotted a crab that looked quite absurd,
"Hey buddy, you're dancing! What's the latest word?"
The crab just grinned with a comical strut,
"Join me in antics, this sea's full of nut!"

"Why not!" laughed the turtle, "Let's groove all day long,

While the ocean hums us a silly old song."
With laughter and fun, the waves became grand,
In the bright blue abyss, they formed a new band!

Beneath the Ebbing Skies

Beneath skies so blue, in a curious zone,
A turtle was lost, all alone with its phone.
It was swiping the waves, looking for a match,
But the only replies were from jellyfish batch.

"Why don't you dive deep?" said a wise ocean fish,
"It's better than swiping, and brighter than a dish!"
With hope in its heart and some sass in its flipper,
It dove to the depths, feeling somewhat crisper.

Through coral and chaos, it twisted and turned,
Found a whole party where excitement had churned.
The fishes were lively, the sea stars so bright,
"Our friend is here—let's dance through the night!"

So the turtle forgot all about its lost quest,
And decided to swim, feeling truly blessed.
A few silly selfies, it bid its farewell,
With stories of fun, in the ocean they dwell!

The Unseen Journey Beyond Shores

A turtle named Timmy, with quite a big dream,
Said, "I'll go beyond where the bright stars gleam!"
With a wink and a nod, it donned a big hat,
And set off in style, feeling dapper and sprat.

The waves played their tricks, and a sly wind blew,
"Hold on to your shell, we've places to view!"
Timmy held tighter while laughing with glee,
"This adventure's a blast, just look at me free!"

It met a crab DJ spinning seashell tunes,
Past fishy conga lines under bright harvest moons.
"Join the fun, dear turtle! Come dance with us now!"
Timmy spun 'round, exclaimed, "Oh wow, oh wow!"

And so they all danced, creating a scene,
With laughter and joy that felt like a dream.
Timmy forgot about shores far away,
In the ocean's embrace, it planned to stay!

The Hidden World Below

In a shell so round, a little guy spins,
He wears the best shades, for sunshine begins.
With flippers that splash, and a wacky dance,
He laughs at the crabs; they just can't prance.

Beneath the bright waves, a party's in sight,
Where fish wear bow ties, oh what a delight!
They wiggle and giggle, all having a blast,
While seaweed shakes hips, it's quite the contrast.

But watch out, dear turtle, for that sneaky shark,
He's plotting a party; it'll leave quite a mark!
With jokes in his gills and tricks in his tail,
He bumbles and fumbles, how can he fail?

Yet tucked in a corner, where currents are meek,
Our turtle stirs up a comedic sneak peek.
He flips and he flops, a show for the crew,
The ocean's a stage, and everyone's due!

In the Embrace of the Tide

The ocean's a playground, so wide and so blue,
With waves that make giggles, for me and for you.
The jellyfish bounce, with umbrellas they glide,
While turtles join in, to surf on the tide.

A flip here, a splash there, it's all in the fun,
The seagulls are laughing, oh what have they done?
They swoop with a cheer, like it's all a grand race,
But the turtles just chuckle, with smiles on their face.

From barnacles' gossip to starfish's sighs,
In this aquatic world, the humor just flies.
With nippers and nibblers, each character's bold,
In the depths of the sea, the funny unfolds.

So let's all dive deep, where the laughter comes near,
Among jests and jives, there's nothing to fear.
With fins all flapping, and all hearts align,
In the sea's warm embrace, life is simply divine!

Shadows Among the Waves

Underneath the surface, where shadows do play,
A turtle will frolic, in a magical way.
He dips in the foam, and then makes a face,
While the dolphins erupt in a splashy embrace.

The octopus giggles, with tentacles wide,
Painting sea murals, while turtles head glide.
With colors so bright, and laughter so loud,
Together they form the silliest crowd.

But who's there lurking, in the depths of the bay?
A crab with a top hat, quite proud in display.
He tries to be fancy, with a suave little bow,
Yet trips on his claws, oh what a show!

So join in the fun, in the ocean's parade,
With a wink and a grin, and a splashy charade.
The shadows have secrets, and stories to share,
In the giggly blue depths, where joy fills the air!

Beneath the Glistening Surf

Beneath the surf gleams, a turtle so stout,
With dreams of adventure, and a funny bout.
He wiggles and jigs, to a buoyant beat,
While the sea cucumbers shuffle their feet.

The sunlight breaks down, like bubbles of gold,
As turtles and fishes spin tales retold.
With tales of the tides and the old sea myths,
They giggle through gills of their briny gifts.

A manta ray joins in, with a cartwheel so slick,
But ends up with kelp, doing quite the trick.
The whole ocean roars, with laughter and cheer,
As the turtle, triumphant, becomes the star here!

So come take a dive, into laughter and cheer,
Where the seashells all whisper, the jokes that we hear.
In the sparkle of ocean, with waves as a guide,
There's humor and joy, in the glistening tide!

www.ingramcontent.com/pod-product-compliance
Lightning Source LLC
Chambersburg PA
CBHW070315120526
44590CB00017B/2682